HORSEPOWER

SPRINT CARS

by Sarah L. Schuette

Reading Consultant:
Barbara J. Fox
Reading Specialist
North Carolina State University

Capstone press®

Mankato, Minnesota

Blazers is published by Capstone Press,
151 Good Counsel Drive, P.O. Box 669, Mankato, Minnesota 56002.
www.capstonepress.com

Library of Congress Cataloging-in-Publication Data
Schuette, Sarah L., 1976–
    Sprint cars / by Sarah L. Schuette.
    p. cm.—(Blazers. Horsepower)
    Includes bibliographical references and index.
    ISBN-13: 978-0-7368-6452-7 (hardcover)
    ISBN-10: 0-7368-6452-0 (hardcover)
    1. Sprint cars—Juvenile literature. I. Title. II. Series.
TL236.27.S38 2007
796.72—dc22   2006000579

Summary: Brief text describes sprint cars, from their design to their
action-packed races.

Editorial Credits
Carrie A. Braulick, editor; Jason Knudson, set designer; Thomas Emery and
    Patrick D. Dentinger, book designers; Jo Miller, photo researcher; Scott
    Thoms, photo editor

Photo Credits
AP Wide World Photos/Tom Kelly, 21
Artemis Images, cover, 12, 14, 15, 16, 20, 22–23
M & M Photos/Matt Sublett, 5, 6, 7, 8, 11, 13, 25, 26, 28–29
TJ Buffenbarger Photo, 19

**Capstone Press thanks Thomas J. Schmeh, Executive Director,
National Sprint Car Hall of Fame & Museum, Knoxville, Iowa, for
his assistance in preparing this book.**

1 2 3 4 5 6 11 10 09 08 07 06

TABLE OF CONTENTS

RIPPING UP THE TRACK

As the race begins, sprint cars speed down the dirt track. The crowd roars with excitement.

5
14
PACIFIC UNION
HOMES
pfi
www.eliteracing.net
Hoosier
Remy
11
Remy
Landscaping
Lafferty
FRAM
MSD
PRO

The cars whip past each other as
they battle for the lead. The driver
in car number 15 makes several
daring passes.

BLAZER FACT

Sprint car races are usually 5 to 30 miles (8 to 48 kilometers) long.

By the last lap, number 15
leads the pack. The bright yellow
car streaks across the finish line.
The driver raises his trophy
and the crowd cheers.

WINGS AND WHEELS

Most sprint cars have wings. These large panels help keep the cars from flying off the track.

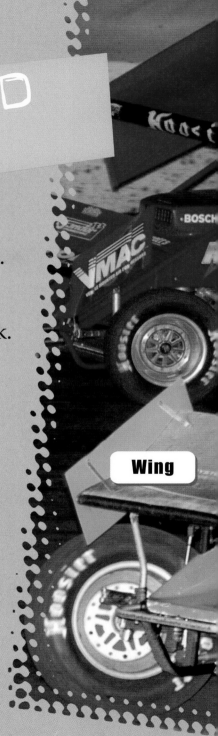

Wing

Wing

Lightweight, hollow pipes form a sprint car frame, or chassis. Most sprint cars weigh about 1,000 pounds (450 kilograms).

BLAZER FACT

Some drivers race sprint cars without wings. These cars are hard to control.

Sprint cars grip dirt tracks with giant back tires. The right rear tire is larger than the left one. This feature helps drivers turn corners.

Engine

Large engines power sprint cars to high speeds. The engine sits in front of the driver.

BLAZER FACT

On some tracks, sprint cars reach 140 miles (225 kilometers) per hour.

SPRINT CARS IN ACTION

All sprint car drivers want to be in the feature race. But they must be a top finisher in heat races first. Every second counts!

BLAZER FACT

A few sprint car races are held indoors on paved tracks.

Racing at high speeds is dangerous. Sprint cars can easily flip. A roll cage around the cockpit protects the driver. A seat belt also keeps the driver safe.

Roll cage

Cockpit

SPRINT CAR PARTS

Wings

Small front tire

Roll cage

Cockpit

Large rear tire

Chassis

TOP DRIVERS

Many top drivers race in the World of Outlaws Sprint Series. In 2005, Steve Kinser became the series champion for the 20th time.

Steve Kinser

Billy Alley is a new driver, but winning isn't new for him. In 2004, he won a rookie of the year award. Alley and other new drivers will keep fans wild about sprint car racing.

BLAZER FACT

In 2002, a video game
based on the World
of Outlaws Series
was released.

Billy Alley

TEARING UP THE TRACK!

GLOSSARY

chassis (CHASS-ee)—the frame on which the body of a vehicle is built

cockpit (KOK-pit)—the area in a sprint car where the driver sits

feature race (FEE-chur RAYSS)—the main race of a sprint car event

heat race (HEET RAYSS)—a race held to determine which drivers will advance to the feature race

roll cage (ROHL KAYJ)—a structure of strong metal tubing in a sprint car that surrounds and protects the driver

rookie (RUK-ee)—a first-year driver

READ MORE

Dubowski, Mark. *Superfast Cars.* Ultimate Speed. New York: Bearport, 2006.

Schaefer, A. R. *Sprint Cars.* Wild Rides! Mankato, Minn.: Capstone Press, 2005.

Sexton, Susan. *Sprint Car Racing: Unleashing the Power.* Cover-to-Cover Books. Logan, Iowa: Perfection Learning, 2003.

INTERNET SITES

FactHound offers a safe, fun way to find Internet sites related to this book. All of the sites on FactHound have been researched by our staff.

Here's how:

1. Visit *www.facthound.com*

2. Choose your grade level.

3. Type in this book ID **0736864520** for age-appropriate sites. You may also browse subjects by clicking on letters, or by clicking on pictures and words.

4. Click on the **Fetch It** button.

FactHound will fetch the best sites for you!

INDEX